The Library of
ASTRONAUT BIOGRAPHIES™

SALLY RIDE

The First American Woman in Space

Tamra Orr

rosen
central™

The Rosen Publishing Group, Inc., New York

Published in 2004 by The Rosen Publishing Group, Inc.
29 East 21st Street, New York, NY 10010

Copyright © 2004 by The Rosen Publishing Group, Inc.

First Edition

Library of Congress Cataloging-in-Publication Data

Orr, Tamra.
Sally Ride : the first American woman in space / Tamra Orr.
    p. cm. — (The library of astronaut biographies)
Summary: A biography of Sally Ride, discussing her early years, education, and career as one of the first women accepted in America's space program.
Includes bibliographical references and index.
ISBN 0-8239-4462-X (library binding)
1. Ride, Sally—Juvenile literature. 2. Astronauts—United States—
Biography—Juvenile literature. 3. Women astronauts—United
States—Biography—Juvenile literature. [1. Ride, Sally. 2. Astronauts.
3. Women—Biography.] I. Title. II. Series.
TL789.85.R53O77 2004
629.45'0092—dc22
                                                    2003014302

Manufactured in the United States of America

CONTENTS

THE DAWN OF THE SPACE AGE

Life in the 1950s was often characterized by change, by the teetering between the traditional past and the technological future. World War II was beginning to fade from people's thoughts only to be replaced by the Cold War between the Soviet Union (modern-day Russia and other newly independent former Soviet republics) and the United States that would feature four decades of simmering tension and a very dangerous and expensive arms race.

In 1951, American schoolchildren practice a "duck and cover" drill that their parents and teachers thought would protect them from the effects of a possible nuclear attack by the Soviet Union.

Family life was changing drastically at this time. The extended families that often lived together in the nation's cities were beginning to go separate ways and move to the suburbs. The nuclear family— a father, mother, and their children—lived apart from grandparents, aunts, uncles, and cousins in new houses in recently built neighborhoods. Though the houses were brand-new, more than a third of them still did not have complete plumbing and were heated by coal rather than gas or electricity. Divorce was much less common than it is today, so most children lived with both of their parents.

Though women had entered the workforce in large numbers during World War II, the return of the soldiers in peacetime meant that many of these women lost or gave up their jobs. In the 1950s, the majority of mothers worked in the home because there were very few jobs considered appropriate for women; there were very few day-care facilities; and being a working mother was often considered unusual or harmful to children. The task deemed most important and appropriate for women was "homemaking"—the creation and managing of a clean, happy, and healthy home for their husbands and children.

Telephones were still making their way into the average home, but, unlike today, homes usually had only one. The days of multiple phone lines, cordless phones, and cell phones were still far in the future. Black-and-white televisions were still a relatively new

In the 1950s, most married women were not in the workforce, and the jobs that were offered tended to be low-level and poorly paid. Many women instead stayed home to undertake the full-time job of child raising and housekeeping.

concept and a rare luxury in many neighborhoods. By the end of the decade, however, almost every home would have one—but only one. The show *I Love Lucy*, starring well-known comedian Lucille Ball, was a huge hit for almost the entire decade. There were only three networks at the time, and they did not broadcast twenty-four hours a day. In 1953, television took on a whole new look when the three networks started broadcasting many of their shows in color.

The jazzy, big-band sound of Frank Sinatra still dominated the radio, but it was beginning to get some stiff competition for young listeners from a new type of music called rock and roll. This rowdy, rhythmic new sound was personified by a shy young man from Biloxi, Mississippi—Elvis Presley—who shook, swayed, and sang in ways many Americans had never seen or heard before. He electrified the teenagers and terrified their parents. A similar generation gap was opening up in the nation's movie theaters and bookstores. The sweet, wholesome Doris Day went head-to-head with the more wild Marilyn Monroe in Hollywood comedies and musicals. Bookstores were selling copies of Dr. Spock's *Baby and Child Care* to the older generation, while the younger generation was snatching up copies of J. D. Salinger's controversial first novel, *The Catcher in the Rye.*

The civil rights movement, which would explode in a series of protests, marches, riots, and court cases all across the country in the 1960s, was already beginning to simmer during the 1950s. In 1954, a landmark court case, *Brown v. Board of Education of Topeka,* ruled in favor of integration of the nation's public schools. It stated that African American children had the legal right to enroll in white public schools in their neighborhoods rather than have to travel miles away to attend "separate but equal" black schools. Despite this historic decision, the battle for equal rights and justice would be fought for many years to come as racism, discrimination, and prejudice continued to exist in the United States.

The world of science was expanding rapidly during this decade. Simple inventions like Tupperware and Velcro were introduced to the country for the first time. More important discoveries included Dr. Jonas Salk's polio vaccine. The solar cell, which can trap and store the Sun's energy and convert it to electricity, was invented at this time, along with the laser and the first computer, called the Univac 1. Automobile production was on the rise, and the country was developing a growing fascination with and dependence upon cars.

One of the most profound changes during the 1950s, however, was a growing desire and ability to travel beyond our planet and explore the mysteries of outer space. The idea of exploring the universe in high-powered rockets had been discussed for years, mostly by science fiction writers like H. G. Wells, Ray Bradbury, and Arthur C. Clarke. The concept was long considered a fantasy by most people. Only a committed and visionary few saw space travel as a legitimate, worthwhile subject of research.

As the Cold War heated up, the United States and the Soviet Union scrambled to keep up with each other's technological advances and weapon development. One avenue of superpower competition that opened up was the "race for space." Both nations entered into a high-stakes battle to be the

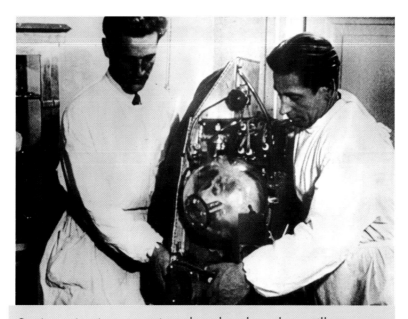

Soviet scientists examine the chamber that will carry a living dog, Laika, up to space on board *Sputnik II*, the second human-made satellite in history. The spaceflight would be an important test of how living beings reacted to the weightless environment of space. *Sputnik II* was launched on November 3, 1957. Laika was supplied with only a week's worth of food and oxygen, however, and died in space before the capsule fell back down to Earth almost six months after its launch.

first to reach space. The Soviets won this battle when they sent up the first artificial satellite, *Sputnik I*, on October 4, 1957. Though *Sputnik* was only a small, harmless metal ball that orbited Earth and sent out a few electronic beeps, it struck terror in the hearts of Americans. They felt they were losing the space race and might soon find themselves targeted by Soviet satellites pointing weapons and spy cameras down at them from the high ground of space.

Sputnik fueled the United States's passion to develop its own national space program. The country felt embarrassed and humiliated to be beaten by the Soviets, and steps were immediately taken to try and catch up to them. In 1958, the National Aeronautics and Space Administration, or NASA, was established to study space exploration and conduct the research that would one day result in the triumphant landing of a man on the Moon.

It was into this exciting era—the dawn of the space age—that future astronaut Sally Kristen Ride was born on May 26, 1951. As a child, she closely followed the progress of the American space program. On April 12, 1961, when she was nine years old, the United States was shaken again when Soviet cosmonaut Yuri Gagarin became the first human being to enter space. ("Cosmonaut" is the Russian term for "astronaut.") Less than a month later, on May 5, the United States countered by sending up Alan Shepard Jr. in the *Mercury 4* space capsule. This first American manned space-flight was only the beginning of a series of increasingly dazzling achievements.

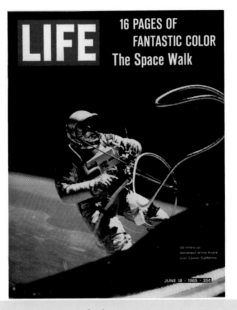

The early achievements of the American space program sparked enthusiastic public interest. NASA astronauts were often profiled in the pages of *Life*, a very popular American weekly magazine that featured large, full-color photographs alongside its reporting. On this cover, Edward White is seen during his *Gemini 4* space walk.

In February 1962, millions of Americans watched on television as John Glenn became the first American to orbit Earth. Like many other fascinated citizens, Ride remembers the precise moment of this historic event, as well as the even more awe-inspiring first Moon landing. She recalled, in Anne E. Schraff's *American Heroes of Exploration and Flight*, "I've always watched the space program closely. I could tell you exactly where I was when John Glenn went into space and when Neil Armstrong walked on the Moon."

Sally Ride had no idea yet that one day she would follow in Glenn's and Armstrong's footsteps. Inspired by these early space pioneers to pursue her interest in science, Ride could not foresee that she would provide similar inspiration to America's youth or that the nation would look to her as one of history's greatest role models for aspiring female scientists and women in general.

CHAPTER 1

TWIN PASSIONS

I n Los Angeles, California, on May 26, 1951, Joyce Ride gave birth to a daughter named Sally. Sally's father, Dr. Dale Ride, was a political science professor at Santa Monica College. Joyce was a stay-at-home mother, as well as a church volunteer, counselor, and part-time English teacher to foreign students. Sally grew up with her family in the Los Angeles suburb of Encino.

By the age of five, before even entering school, Sally had already taught herself how to read. Her favorite books were mysteries and spy stories, especially those that featured detective Nancy

Drew and special agent James Bond. An enthusiastic sports fan, Sally pored over the sports pages of the newspaper, memorizing the daily scores.

When she was not reading about sports, she was often playing them. Softball was her favorite sport as a young child, and she was the only girl who was allowed to play on the all-boys' neighborhood softball and football teams. Learning that a girl can be a welcome and valuable part of a primarily male team was something she would always remember and appreciate. This early experience of crossing the boundaries that often separate men and women would serve Sally well in adult life as she continually fought to make a place for herself in traditionally male-dominated fields.

Meeting the Wider World

Throughout Sally's childhood, her parents made a point of exposing her and her sister, Karen, to other countries, cultures, and people. Her parents valued education and exploration and were very supportive of their daughters' interests and pursuits. "My parents must have done a great job. Anytime I wanted to pursue something that they weren't familiar with, that was not part of their lifestyle," Ride says in Chris Crocker's *Great American Astronauts*, "they let me go ahead and do it." Joyce puts it this way in Jane and Sue Hurwitz's *Sally Ride*: "Dale and I simply forgot to tell them that there were things they couldn't do. But I think if it occurred to us to tell them, we would have refrained . . . We didn't talk a lot about careers because we didn't want to pressure them into anything specific."

In addition to this open and encouraging attitude, Sally's parents also traveled a great deal. When Sally was nine, Dale took a leave of absence from work. The entire family then spent a year in Europe. Dale and Joyce home-schooled the girls while they were on the road. Once they returned from the year abroad, both of the Ride girls were ahead in all of their classes. The Ride family also hosted a number of visitors from other countries, further educating the girls on how other people lived and opening their eyes to the wide range of possibilities that life offers. These were lessons that would stay with Sally for the rest of her life.

Dividing Her Time

Sally's interest in sports continued to grow as she got older. When she was ten years old, she began playing tennis and was coached by Alice Marble, a four-time women's national champion. Although she participated in a number of sports, by the time Sally was in high school, tennis had become her clear favorite. In her junior year, she was already the eighteenth-ranked junior player in the United States. At age twenty-two, she received personal encouragement to turn professional from female tennis star and Wimbledon champion Billie Jean King.

Her dedication to tennis, however, was at odds with her second interest—science. As she went through Westlake, an all-girls' private high school in Los Angeles, she received straight As in all of her classes and graduated as one of the school's top six students. Though she excelled in all her subjects and had wide-ranging interests, her academic preference was clearly science. "I probably knew that [I wanted to be a scientist] by seventh or eighth grade. I knew that my interests in science were there," says Ride. In *Portraits of Great American Scientists*, she noted, "I do not know whether I would have been able to

A young Sally Ride is seen here in 1968, posing for her senior portrait. She would graduate that year from the Westlake School for Girls, in Los Angeles, California. One of her class's top six students, she was also an extremely talented athlete. After graduation, she briefly considered pursuing a professional tennis career.

verbalize [my interests] then. I was reading *Scientific American,* and science classes and math classes were my favorite classes. I knew pretty early that I was interested in science."

During her junior year in high school, Ride met a teacher who would have an enormous influence on her. Her name was Dr. Elizabeth Mommaerts, and she taught physiology. It was Mommaerts who introduced Ride to the scientific method—learning to solve a problem through close observation and experimental tests. Anytime Ride observed something that she did not understand, she learned how to answer her own questions by forming a theory that would explain the mystery. She would test the theory by gathering information and then draw conclusions based on her observations that would either support her theory or contradict it and point her in a new direction. This scientific method was not unlike the detective work performed by her role model, Nancy Drew, and its combination of hard science and mystery solving greatly appealed to Ride. It taught her to love the process of solving problems, a skill she would use a great deal in her professional life.

Soon Mommaerts became Ride's new real-life role model. "She was obviously intelligent, clear thinking, and extremely logical," says Ride about her lifelong friend in Carole Ann Camp's *Sally Ride*. "I had never seen logic personified before." Mommaerts admired Ride quite a bit, too, and was the first person to really encourage her to pursue a career in science. Later in life, Ride dedicated her memoir, *To Space and Back*, in part to this special teacher and mentor.

It was quite difficult for Ride to balance her two very different passions. "I spent a lot of time playing and practicing tennis, and I also spent a lot of time with my schoolwork," she explains in *Portraits of Great American Scientists*. After she graduated from Westlake, she found herself increasingly torn between pursuing sports or academics. Eventually, science would take precedence over tennis, but it was an extremely difficult decision. In the end, Ride concluded that her skill in science was greater than her talent for tennis. "Sally simply couldn't make the ball go just where she wanted it to go," recalls Joyce Ride in Schraff's *American Heroes of Exploration and Flight*. "And Sally wouldn't settle for anything short of excellence in herself."

CHAPTER 2

FINDING HER PATH

After Sally Ride graduated from high school, it was time to move on to college. Still torn between the choice of a career in tennis or science, Ride tried to juggle them both and found herself waffling back and forth several times. Twice before she enrolled in college and once afterward, she seriously considered becoming a professional tennis player. Each time, however, she changed her mind and returned to her studies.

Ride began her college education in 1968 at a small liberal arts university called Swarthmore College, just outside Philadelphia, Pennsylvania.

Within her first two years there, she quickly became known as an excellent athlete and won back-to-back crowns in the Eastern Intercollegiate Women's Tennis Championships. Upset, however, that Swarthmore did not have indoor courts and she could not play tennis year-round, Ride decided to leave college and, for the very last time, pursue the possibility of a professional career in tennis. She decided to launch her tennis career back in her home state of sunny California, a climate friendly to year-round tennis.

It would prove to be a very short career. "In my sophomore year of college," Ride explains in *Portraits of Great American Scientists*, "I had a change of heart and decided to give tennis a serious try, and fortunately, that only lasted a couple of months. I went back to school and that was pretty much it." This was by no means an end to her love of sports and physical activity, however. Although she had made the decision once and for all to pursue her studies in science, transferring to Stanford University near San Francisco, she continued to keep herself in shape by running 5 miles (8 kilometers) a day, playing rugby, and participating in various informal campus sports.

Keeping an Eye on NASA

As she went through college, Ride kept a close eye on the amazing advances being made within the NASA space program following the Moon landings of the recently completed Apollo missions. Having conquered the Moon, NASA was looking to take manned space exploration in a different direction. In 1972, President Richard Nixon authorized NASA to begin the research and development of the space shuttle program. The space shuttle was designed to be the world's first reusable spacecraft, a multiuser vehicle that could ferry supplies to space stations, carry satellites and space-based tele-scopes into orbit, and conduct experiments in a large cargo bay laboratory. In addition, in 1973, *Skylab*, the United States's first orbiting space station, was launched.

Both of these new projects were of great interest to scientists and the American public in the 1970s, a time when enthusiasm for the space program was beginning to wane. With the triumph of the Apollo Moon landings already receding into the past and with the Vietnam War and the Watergate presidential scandal distracting and upsetting the nation, the space program seemed less and less like a priority. NASA hoped to reignite the nation's curiosity, imagination, and passion for exploration by taking the next great leap forward and proving that it was possible to live and work in outer space for long periods of time.

Graduate Work

Ride graduated from Stanford in June 1973 with a bachelor of science degree in physics and a bachelor of arts degree in English—a rather unusual combination of studies. During her college years, she discovered that she had a real fascination with the works of English playwright William Shakespeare. She briefly considered going to graduate school for Shakespearean studies. "I really had fun reading Shakespeare's plays and writing papers on them," she says in *American Heroes of Exploration and Flight*. "It's kind of like doing puzzles. You had to figure out what he was trying to say and find all the little clues inside the play that [proved] you were right." Even in her literary pursuits, Ride was applying the

This is a photograph of the campus of Stanford University, in California. Sally Ride received two undergraduate degrees—in physics and English literature—from Stanford in 1973 and immediately returned to begin her graduate studies in astrophysics. Eighteen NASA astronauts, including Ride, have degrees from Stanford University.

scientific method taught to her by Dr. Mommaerts at Westlake to solve difficult puzzles.

Three months after graduation, Ride returned to Stanford University to begin advanced graduate work in astrophysics—the study of the movement and behavior of objects in space. Two years later, in 1975, Ride received her master's degree in physics.

To qualify as a full-fledged astrophysicist, however, she needed a doctoral degree, so she stayed in graduate school for three more years. Finally, in 1978, Ride graduated with a Ph.D. in astrophysics and went on to write a number of important papers on various kinds of lasers.

At this point, Ride's career plan was fairly straightforward—to find work somewhere within the field of physics. Despite her youthful interest in the American space program, becoming an astronaut simply had not occurred to her. "I was interested in space, but it wasn't anything I built a career around," she explains in the Hurwitzes' *Sally Ride*. "Instead I planned to go into research in physics. I wouldn't have known how to prepare for a career as an astronaut even if it had occurred to me to try, since women weren't involved in the space program at that time." Though Ride was unaware of it, all of that was about to change dramatically.

Answering NASA's Call

While she was still working on her Ph.D. at Stanford in the mid-1970s, Ride happened to see

THE FIRST WOMAN IN SPACE

Although Sally Ride would one day become the first American woman in space, the very first woman to leave Earth's atmosphere was Soviet cosmonaut Valentina Tereshkova. In her younger years, Tereshkova had worked as a technician in cotton mills. In her spare time, she had made several parachute jumps and dreamed of one day going into space. Eventually, she was accepted into the Soviet space program. In June 1963, her dream finally came true. Riding in the space capsule *Vostok 6*, Tereshkova was sent into space on a three-day mission.

At the end of the flight, Tereshkova ejected from the capsule 4.2 miles (6.8 km) above the ground and parachuted down to Earth. She immediately became a national hero in the Soviet Union.

a notice in the campus newspaper, *The Stanford Daily*, stating that NASA was searching for scientists who were interested in becoming mission specialists. It had been ten years since NASA had recruited on such a large scale. To Ride's further surprise, NASA stated that they were encouraging women to apply for these positions. This was a first! Ride decided to send in an application, along with her health records and letters of reference. It was a decision that would dramatically change her life.

Sally Ride was not the only person to spot NASA's call for applicants and send in her name for consideration. In fact, 8,369 other people did the same thing; more than 1,000 of them were women. In October 1977, only 208 of these thousands of applicants were chosen and asked to come in for interviews and examinations. The screening process was very rigorous. NASA candidates had to be in excellent shape and had to meet certain physical requirements. For example, they had to be less than forty years old, taller than 5 feet (1.5 meters), but shorter than 6 feet 2 inches (1.9 m). Their eyesight had to be at least 20/100.

The mental and emotional health of the astronaut candidates were as great a consideration for NASA as was their physical health. Floating in zero gravity within cramped quarters for a week or more could be a very disorienting and stressful experience, as could any life-threatening emergencies that might pop up at any time during a spaceflight. NASA needed astronauts who would always keep their cool, solve unexpected problems, and work well and in close quarters with others. Psychologists put the candidates through a series of long and involved interviews, which included questions about their background, education, hobbies, research, and political beliefs. "We saw two psychiatrists for about forty-five minutes each," recalls Ride in the Hurwitzes' *Sally Ride*. "One of them was generally exactly what I had always pictured from a psychiatrist—[a person] who showed you the comfortable chair . . . and then asked you how you felt about your sister. Then the other . . . was sort of the bad guy psychiatrist, who tried to rattle you."

The NASA applicants also had to undergo many physical and mental stress tests. The committee who graded the astronaut candidates was looking less at

This 1978 NASA portrait of Sally Ride was taken when she was still an astronaut candidate. She was accepted into the space program on January 16, 1978. After three years of training, Ride received her first mission assignment in April 1981, providing weather information to a *Columbia* shuttle crew during their descent to Earth.

how they accomplished the given tasks and more at how they reacted to the stress of the situation. Complete physical examinations were also given, including a treadmill test to check heart function.

From the original group of 208 candidates, 35 people made the final cut and joined NASA as astronaut trainees. One of those 35 was Ride. On January 16, 1978, Ride received her call of acceptance from George Abbey, a NASA official. "Well, we've got a job here for you if you are still interested in taking it," he said. She was absolutely thrilled. She immediately called her mother to share the news. "It didn't even occur to me that I'd get accepted," she says in the Hurwitzes' *Sally Ride*. Not only would Sally Ride be accepted into NASA, she would soon become its most famous, beloved, and inspiring astronaut.

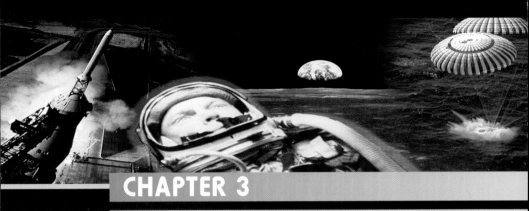

CHAPTER 3

SALLY RIDE, ASTRONAUT

Sally Ride entered NASA with thirty-four other trainees. Of this group, five others were women. Her female peers included Anna Fisher, a medical doctor; Shannon Lucid, a chemist; Margaret Seddon, a surgeon; Kathryn Sullivan, a geologist; and Judith Resnik, an electrical engineer. Ride was delighted to be entering the space program with other accomplished and talented women. "I thought it was very wise of NASA and demonstrated that they had a real commitment to bringing women into the astronaut corps when they brought six of us in at once," says Ride in *Great American Astronauts*. "Of course, there is security in

The first six women to be accepted into NASA's astronaut trainee program pose before a model of the space shuttle. From left to right are Margaret Seddon, Anna Fisher, Judith Resnick, Shannon Lucid, Sally Ride, and Kathryn Sullivan. They entered NASA as part of a class of thirty-five astronaut candidates.

numbers. When you're one out of thirty-five you can be considered a token; when there are six out of thirty-five, it's obvious that the program is committed to including women and that any issues that might arise just have to be dealt with because this is the way things are going to be."

Ride was uncomfortable, however, with the amount of media attention she received for being one of the first women chosen to participate in the American space program. "I did not come to NASA to make history," she says in *Great American Astronauts*. "It's important to me that people don't think I was picked for the flight because I was a woman and it's time for NASA to send one." Throughout her career at NASA, Ride never felt at ease being the center of attention.

When Ride was selected by NASA, she said, "It's too bad that society isn't to the point yet where the country could just end up with a woman astronaut and nobody would think twice about it" (as quoted in *Great American Astronauts*). When women astronauts were first permitted to go on missions, there was some unhappiness about it within NASA. Alan Bean, an Apollo and *Skylab* veteran, is quoted in Camp's *Sally Ride*, "At first, I imagined they [women] were just individuals trying to do a man's job." However, he changed his opinion later. "I was proven wrong . . . Females intuitively understand astronaut skills. They perform the mental and physical tasks as well as men."

Throughout the 1970s, national attention was often riveted on the issue of women's rights. Efforts to promote equality in the workplace and gain the states' approval for the Equal Rights Amendment passed by both houses of Congress in 1972 kept the topic in the news. This public interest in equal rights for women was one of the main reasons behind NASA's decision to accept applications from female scientists. According to Carolyn Huntoon, the Johnson Space Center's deputy chief of personnel, there were other reasons as well. "Because we had a new spacecraft [the space shuttle] and it was going to be built so that it had space inside it . . . and could have toilet facilities that could accommodate women . . . and I think, because at that time in our country, people were feeling a little bit bad about the way they treated women . . . they said, 'It's a federal job and we're going to open it to all races, sexes, religious back-grounds, and ages,'" she recalls in the Hurwitzes' *Sally Ride.*

Since those early days of exclusion, women have become commonplace in NASA. In 1999, United States Air Force lieutenant colonel Eileen Marie Collins became the first woman to hold the position of space shuttle pilot and the first woman to command a space shuttle.

Just as women proved they could work side by side with men in the rigorous, high-pressure atmosphere of astronaut training and space-flight, they also have proved they are every bit as courageous and heroic as their male counter-parts and prepared to face the most extreme dangers. Four women have died during NASA shuttle missions. On January 28, 1986, Sharon Christa McAuliffe—who would have been the first school teacher to go to space—and Judith Resnik were killed when the space shuttle *Challenger* exploded soon after takeoff. In early 2003, NASA lost two more of its female astro-nauts. On February 1, the space shuttle *Columbia*—the oldest craft in the shuttle fleet—broke apart during reentry into Earth's atmosphere after a successful and largely trouble-free mission. On board were the United States's Laurel Clark and India's Kalpana Chawla, along with five other crew members. All are thought to have died instantly.

In general, however, Ride found NASA's attitude toward her and her fellow women trainees refreshingly straightforward and fair-minded. "The attitude of both men and women in the astronaut program was not, were you a man or woman, but could you do the job?" she explains in *Great American Astronauts*. "We are really all very similar," she adds in reference to the group of trainees. "We're all people who are dedicated to the space program and who really want to fly in the space shuttle. That's a common characteristic that we all have that transcends the different backgrounds."

Astronaut Training

The year of astronaut training was intimidating, exhausting, and intense. Ride ran 4 miles (6.4 km) a day and twice that much on weekends. She lifted weights and played tennis and volleyball. In addition to physical training, she and the other trainees were also drilled in the technical aspects of spaceflight. They received training in all of the various shuttle systems, such as the electrical, mechanical, guidance, propulsion, and climate control systems, and how

Sally Ride is seen here in the shuttle mission simulator (SMS). The simulator allows astronauts to prepare for actual shuttle missions by providing them with a mock-up that duplicates all of the shuttle's controls and instruments. They are able to experience a wide range of conditions and situations that might occur on a real mission. Usually, an entire crew will work in the simulator together, with each person performing the tasks that will be assigned to him or her when in space.

they interacted with each other. They also learned how to handle system failures and other emergencies. Each shuttle crew member would have to know how to perform the tasks assigned to all his or her fellow crew members so that if someone could no longer perform his or her job for any reason during a mission, another astronaut could easily take over and prevent an emergency. For this reason, the amount of information the trainees had to absorb and remember was overwhelming.

One of the most important elements of the training program was preparation for working in

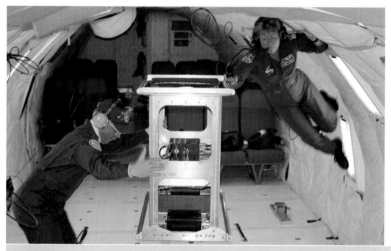

Two astronaut candidates receive weightlessness training in a KC-135 transport plane, better known as the vomit comet. During a steep descent from an equally steep climb, a brief sensation of weightlessness is created, allowing trainees to become more familiar with how it feels to move around and perform tasks in zero gravity.

the zero gravity of space—weightlessness. To simulate this unique sensation, astronaut trainees had to wear scuba gear and enter buoyancy chambers—large tanks filled with water. The feeling of moving slowly and steadily underwater is a close match for the weightless conditions in space and one of the best ways to simulate zero gravity while still in Earth's heavy atmosphere. While underwater, the trainees practiced everything from putting on their space suits to moving equipment around.

Another way to simulate weightless conditions while still in Earth's atmosphere is to take a ride in NASA's KC-135 transport plane, lovingly nick-named the "vomit comet." Inside this specially outfitted plane, the walls are padded and there are no seats. The pilots of the KC-135 gain altitude in a steep climb at high speed. As they reach the peak of the plane's arc, they begin a controlled and steep dive. For about thirty seconds, as the KC-135 is at the top of its arc and beginning to descend, the passengers experience weightless conditions. The sensation is that of a very wild, very long, and steep plunge on a roller coaster, when you are lifted out of your seat and your stomach feels as if it is rising to your throat. Astronaut trainees usually have to endure thirty or more of these arcing dives in a single flight.

Some of the astronauts cope well with this sensation; others experience air sickness and a feeling of disorientation or confusion. Ride was not bothered by the wild ride. "About 40 to 50 percent of the astronauts do get sick, and 50 to 60 percent don't, and I was one of the lucky ones," she explains in the Hurwitzes' *Sally Ride*. "[Astronauts] feel like they're hanging from the ceiling and the Earth is in the wrong place. Some people say they almost feel drugged, they're so tired," she adds. "Generally [the feeling] lasts about two days."

Training did not end with the vomit comet. Even more rigorous exercises awaited the astronaut trainees. They went scuba diving in icy waters and rode rafts on rocky seas. Ride and her fellow trainees also endured a "drop and drag" exercise. While wearing their space suits, astronauts were strapped into opened parachutes and then dropped into water from a moving boat. Astronauts had to be able to free themselves from the parachute harnesses while being dragged on their stomachs and backs.

Astronaut candidate Eileen Collins climbs out of the pool during a water survival training exercise at the Naval Air Station in Pensacola, Florida. Shuttle astronauts have to receive water survival training in case of any accidents during launch or reentry that may force a crash landing into the ocean.

Once freed, they had to swim—still weighed down by their heavy, bulky space suits—to a nearby dock. This exercise was exhausting and often scary, but it also helped teach the trainees how to cope with an emergency water landing.

In addition to these often torturous physical tests and simulations, an enormous amount of time was spent on practical instrument training. Each trainee spends twelve to fifteen hours per week in the space shuttle simulator learning what each and every button and lever does and when they should and should not be used.

Beyond the demanding physical and practical training, there were also endless meetings. "People think we're tossed into centrifuges,

Public relations—which involves things like giving interviews to reporters, speeches to politicians and businesspeople, and presentations to schoolchildren— is a very large part of an astronaut's job. Because Sally Ride was one of NASA's first female astronauts, she spent more time in front of the cameras and microphones than most astronauts.

dunked into water, and thrown out of planes in this work," says Ride in the Hurwitzes' *Sally Ride*, "but it's not always exciting. We sit behind desks and go to meetings mostly." Some of these meetings were seminars on effective public speaking, offering tips on how to field the many questions each astronaut would eventually be asked by the media. Public relations is an extremely important part of an astronaut's job. Because NASA depends upon government funding and taxpayer support to carry out its missions, it must continuously explain the importance of its work and keep the public interested in and supportive of its programs.

All in all, astronaut trainees usually put in at least sixty hours a week of very difficult and tiring work. When the training period was finally over and the candidates became full-fledged astronauts, they were all enormously relieved, including Ride.

Waiting Her Turn and Working Hard

After the so-called TFNG—thirty-five new guys— had completed their training, they were ready to go

A SPACE AGE ROMANCE

One of Ride's fellow astronaut trainees was Dr. Steven A. Hawley. He had a Ph.D. in astronomy from the University of California at Santa Cruz. He and Ride got to know each other during the training period, and on July 24, 1982, they were married. They became one of three astronaut couples within the space program. Their wedding was a simple and casual one, held at Hawley's parents' home in Salina, Kansas. Ride flew herself there in a small airplane and was wed wearing a pair of jeans and a plain shirt. Two ministers performed the ceremony, Dr. Bernard Hawley, Steven's father, and Reverend Karen Scott, Ride's sister. After they were married, they moved into a home not far from the Johnson Space Center in Houston, Texas. They decorated their home with a variety of NASA souvenirs, from posters and shuttle dishware to photographs of the Moon landing. Ride and Hawley's marriage was a brief one, however. They divorced in 1987 but remained good friends.

into space. But who would go first, and when? Other established astronauts were ahead of them on the mission waiting list, and they would have to wait their turns.

In the meantime, Ride and the others were assigned to SAIL, the Shuttle Avionics Integration Laboratory. SAIL ran twenty-four hours a day, seven days a week. The astronauts worked eight-hour shifts, examining the parts of the shuttle and how they worked, testing new procedures, and simulating problems to see how they could be solved. The laboratory featured duplicates, or copies, of the shuttle cockpits. Ride spent many hours in these simulators, learning about potential crises and sharpening her emergency responses and problem-solving skills. The simulator sessions were videotaped so that each of the astronauts' reactions and decisions could be studied and evaluated later. The simulators provided the new astronauts with a valuable hands-on education. They helped ensure that the rookies would not be surprised by anything once they finally got their chance to soar into space. "We have a simulator in Houston that's very good," says Ride in the

Hurwitzes' *Sally Ride.* "They turn you on your back and shake you and vibrate you and pump noise in, so that it's very realistic."

In addition to the time spent in SAIL, each of the candidates also spent hours learning to fly the T-38 training jet. This is the plane that flies alongside the shuttle on its way to a safe runway landing after it reenters Earth's atmosphere. Flight training familiarized Ride with cockpit controls and displays, as well as the sensation of traveling at high speeds within a very small space. Unlike the early generations of NASA astronauts, not all the new recruits were drawn from the military, so piloting was often a brand-new experience for them.

Zooming around in the T-38s also gave the new astronauts the opportunity to see what the heavy pull of gravity felt like during rapid acceleration—not an entirely pleasant sensation. During takeoff and reentry, astronauts would experience roughly five to seven Gs (a G refers to gravitational force). This means they would be laboring under five to seven times the force of gravity usually experienced on Earth. That kind of pressure makes it difficult to

An astronaut trainee *(seated at left)* prepares for a training flight on board a T-38 jet. Flying in these jets gave NASA candidates valuable flying and piloting experience. In addition, these speedy jets helped astronaut trainees prepare for the physical stresses of spaceflight. T-38s generate five to seven Gs when they accelerate, similar to the amount of gravitational force placed on astronauts during a shuttle's takeoff and reentry.

move and can cause dizziness, disorientation, and even loss of consciousness.

As always, Ride was exhilarated rather than intimidated by this training. In fact, she enjoyed it so much that she went on to earn a pilot's license.

Ride's First Assignment

Finally, after the many long, grueling months of training and working at SAIL, Ride received her first mission assignment. Though this first job would not take her into space, she would serve a very important role on the ground in several shuttle missions, paving the way for her own first space-flight. Ride was assigned the position of mission specialist, a job that requires a college degree in science or engineering and at least three years in a specialty (astrophysics, in Ride's case). The mission specialist must know about every aspect of each shuttle operation and take in-depth courses in basic sciences, guidance and navigation, meteorology, astronomy, computers, physics, and math.

Ride played a role in the first three flights of the space shuttle *Columbia*. During its maiden, or first, voyage in April 1981, she rode in the T-38 chase plane as *Columbia* began to reenter Earth's atmosphere. She was responsible for providing weather information to the shuttle crew during their descent and taking pictures of the landing. During *Columbia*'s second and third missions, in the fall and winter of 1981, Ride

A T-38 chase plane is seen here observing the launch of the space shuttle *Columbia* on March 22, 1982. The photo was taken from the cockpit of another T-38 chase plane. In the early days of the Shuttle program, the T-38s shadowed the space shuttle during takeoff and landing, providing shuttle crews with weather information and taking pictures of the craft in case NASA should need to investigate any problems that may have occurred during a mission. Those planes still accompany the shuttles during landing.

worked as the capcom, or capsule communicator. The capcom is considered the voice of mission control during a mission, and it is an extremely important position. Only one person on Earth is allowed to talk directly with the shuttle crew during a spaceflight. This helps prevent the crew from becoming overwhelmed with or confused by comments and instructions coming from multiple voices. As capcom, Ride answered the crew's questions, gave them important information, and delivered the flight director's instructions. She was the first woman to ever shoulder this awesome responsibility.

 Sally Ride is seen in this 1981 photograph serving as capcom during a simulation of STS-2, the second shuttle mission in history. As capcom, she would be the one person responsible for relaying information between mission control and the shuttle crew. She would perform this job during STS-3 as well. Ride was the first woman ever to be appointed as capcom.

In addition to her responsibilities as mission specialist and capcom, Sally Ride also worked extensively on the development of the remote manipulator system (RMS)—a large robotic arm housed in the shuttle's cargo bay. The RMS has a bend in the middle similar to an elbow—only this "elbow" allows the arm to bend in four different directions. The arm has a clawlike hand that rotates at the end, like a wrist, and grasps satellites or other heavy but delicate equipment and machinery.

The RMS can pluck a satellite out of storage in the shuttle's cargo bay and lift it away from the shuttle out into space, where it will then be placed into orbit. The RMS also helps build space structures, load or unload equipment, and retrieve older satellites for repair or return to Earth. The RMS is capable of handling payloads as heavy as 65,000 pounds (29,484 kilograms). It is a very important part of the equipment that is helping to build and maintain the International Space Station (ISS), a large international laboratory that orbits Earth and is a temporary home and office to visiting astronaut-scientists who conduct research in space.

With every shuttle flight in which she participated on the ground, Ride was moving closer to discovering for herself what outer space was like. Finally, the word came down from NASA administrators—Ride was assigned to shuttle mission STS-7 as mission specialist. She would be going into space in June 1983 on the space shuttle *Challenger*. Soon,

Following the successful completion of STS-3, NASA's third shuttle mission, Sally Ride reviews postflight data on the mission at the Johnson Space Center in Houston in April 1982. As capcom for this mission, Ride would meet with mission control and the shuttle crew to compare notes about the mission and evaluate what things worked and what things didn't.

Sally Ride would become the first American woman to travel beyond Earth's atmosphere!

The entire crew was carefully selected. It included shuttle commander Robert Crippen (the pilot of the very first space shuttle mission in 1981), shuttle pilot Frederick Hauck, mission specialist John Fabian, Dr. Norman Thagard (a physician), and Ride. To counter any suggestion by the media that Ride's participation was a publicity stunt or a token gesture toward women's equality, Crippen is quoted in *Great American Astronauts* as saying, "She is flying with us because she is the very best person for the job. There is no man I would rather have in her place. You like people who stay calm under duress [stressful situations]. And Sally can do that." The STS-7 mission featured the largest crew that NASA had ever sent into orbit. With Ride aboard, it was destined to make even greater history.

CHAPTER 4

RIDE, SALLY, RIDE!

After five long and grueling years of training, studying, and patiently waiting, Sally Ride's time had finally come—the countdown to her first shuttle flight. On June 18, 1983, at 7:33 AM, the space shuttle *Challenger* took off from Florida's Cape Canaveral, carrying not only four satellites but also the first American woman to journey beyond Earth's atmosphere. The public areas surrounding the launch site were crowded with journalists, cameras, film crews, and an enthusiastic and supportive public. More than 1,000 reporters were on hand to record the moment. Spectators urged the nation's first female astronaut to "Ride, Sally, Ride!" More than half a million spectators watched the event—including Ride's parents and husband.

As the moment of liftoff approached, the tension mounted inside the shuttle. Each member of the crew was strapped down in a seat. They were lying on their backs, and their feet were just slightly higher than their heads. Ride watched the blinking lights and flashing

Sally Ride *(left)* and fellow crew members Robert Crippen *(right)*, John Fabian *(rear)*, and Norman Thagard *(behind Fabian)* prepare to enter the shuttle *Challenger* before the launch of STS-7.

numbers on the control board and reported what she saw to Crippen. Suddenly, the space shuttle began to shudder as the engines roared to life and Earth began to fall away beneath them. It was not a smooth ride. As Crippen described it in *The Greatest Adventure* by Ingaret Ward, "The ride on the first stage with the solids [the shuttle's two solid

The space shuttle *Challenger* lifts off at 7:33 AM on June 18, 1983, from Cape Canaveral, Florida. This was NASA's seventh shuttle launch and the second flight of *Challenger*. The crew's commander, Robert Crippen, became the first astronaut to fly on the shuttle twice. He had piloted the very first space shuttle flight.

rocket boosters] is like driving a pickup truck down an old washboard country road." Despite the bumps, Ride and her fellow crew members were thrilled and exhilarated. The moment they had all worked so hard and long for was finally here—liftoff!

The View from Up There

Liftoff was an awe-inspiring moment for Sally Ride. "The engines light, the solids light, and all of a sudden, you know you are going. It's overwhelming. There is nothing like it," she says in *Great American Astronauts*. She was thrust back into her seat by three times the force of gravity for several minutes but remained cool and calm, despite the crushing G forces and the adrenaline rush.

Seeing Earth begin to fall away beneath her was an awe-inspiring sight for Ride. "You spend a year training just which dials to look at and when the time comes," she says in Carole S. Briggs's *Women in Space*, "all you want to do is look out the window. It's so beautiful!" Although she had work to do and jobs to perform, Ride was briefly overwhelmed by the entire liftoff experience.

This picture of the space shuttle *Challenger* was taken by the shuttle pallet satellite (SPAS), an orbiting laboratory platform that can conduct experiments in space. The SPAS had just been released from the shuttle's cargo bay during STS-7. The robotic arm that lifted it out of the bay can be seen to the left and just below the shuttle's cockpit. Earth, under cloud cover, can be seen below the shuttle.

Despite all the zero-gravity training the crew had received, it was still rather difficult to get used to this new sensation of floating. Although Ride enjoyed the sensation, it took some time for her to learn how to deal with it. She had to learn to move from place to place by pushing off of things—but not too hard, because then she would crash into something on the other side of the orbiter. "I constantly felt that I was about to lose control, as though I were teetering on a balance beam or tipping over in a canoe," she says in Camp's *Sally Ride*. "It's a strange, unsteady feeling that's difficult to describe, but fortunately goes away." She goes on to describe in an interview with Scholastic.com just what moving around the shuttle was like. "It doesn't feel any different to your body or your insides," she says. "So you feel the same. But the difference is that you can float in the middle of the room—you can do somersaults in the middle of the room, and in fact, you can't stand on the floor. You will float off the floor."

Getting Down to Work

The shuttle's flight lasted six days, two hours, and twenty-three minutes. The *Challenger* orbited Earth a total of ninety-eight times. Its cargo bay carried two communication satellites that were to be released into orbit. One was called the *Palapa B-2,*

Sally Ride's First Spaceflight

Only eight and a half thunderous minutes after launch, I was orbiting high above Earth, suddenly able to watch typhoons form, volcanoes smolder, and meteors streak through the atmosphere below. In orbit, racing along at 5 miles [8 km] per second, the space shuttle circles Earth once every ninety minutes. If I turned my concentration away from the window for too long, I could miss an entire land mass . . . We could see smoke rising from fires that dotted the entire east coast of Africa, and in the same orbit only moments later, ice floes jostling for position in the Antarctic. We could see the Ganges River dumping its murky, sediment-laden water into the Indian Ocean and watch ominous hurricane clouds expanding and rising like biscuits in the oven of the Caribbean.

—Sally Ride, from Ingaret Ward's
The Greatest Adventure

an Indonesian satellite. The other was the *Anik-C*, a Canadian satellite. It was Ride's job to deploy, or place, these two satellites into space, using the RMS that she had trained on for so many hours. By relaying telephone signals from one part of the world to another, these satellites would help to connect millions of people around the globe.

In addition to this job, Ride also participated in and monitored forty different experiments, some of which were "getaway specials"—experiments designed to take advantage of the shuttle's "getaway" from Earth's gravity into weightless conditions. Some of the experiments were suggested by college and even high school students; others were designed by private companies and government agencies. The sponsors pay between $3,000 and $10,000 to have their experiments performed in space. One experiment designed by high school students from Camden, New Jersey, involved studying the differing effects of gravity and weightlessness on a colony of 150 carpenter ants. Another experiment from students at the California Technical Institute explored the effects of zero gravity on the growth of radish seeds. If there is no up or down in space and no force like gravity pushing something in a certain direction, which way would the seeds send their roots?

On the fifth day of the mission, Ride used the RMS for a new purpose. This time, instead of only deploying a satellite, she would also attempt to retrieve, or capture, one. This would help establish the space shuttle's usefulness in salvaging dead satellites and fixing broken ones. Several hours after deploying a West German shuttle pallet satellite (SPAS), Ride used the robot arm to retrieve it and haul it back into the cargo bay. SPAS satellites are reusable and can function while sitting in the cargo bay or when floating free in space. They usually contain sensors for observation of space or Earth's atmosphere. They also serve as floating labs, carrying a series of experiments that rely on zero gravity for their results. The SPAS that Ride retrieved contained both space observation devices and ten experiments involving the formation of metal alloys in zero gravity. The satellite's retrieval and placement in the shuttle's cargo bay went off perfectly. Shuttle commander Crippen responded to the successful operation with an amused, "We pick up and deliver."

Sally Ride monitors control panels from the pilot's chair on the *Challenger*'s flight deck during STS-7. STS-7 was a very busy mission, with a full schedule of jobs to perform. Ride enjoyed very little free time and had to remain focused on her work, not on the scenery outside the shuttle window.

The shuttle's robotic arm approaches the shuttle pallet satellite (SPAS) in preparation for a deployment and retrieval test. During STS-7, Ride would deploy two other satellites with the help of the robotic arm.

Life in Space

Life on the space shuttle was both fascinating and challenging. Each crew member was kept constantly busy with a strict schedule of duties to perform. There was very little time to just sit and relax and watch the stunning scenery go by. When the day was over and it was time to go to bed, each crew member had found a slightly different way to sleep in zero gravity. Ride chose to sleep in a rather unique way. "Different astronauts sleep in different ways," she explains in the Scholastic.com interview. "I slept just floating in the middle of the flight deck, the upper deck of the space shuttle. Some astronauts sleep in sort of beds—compartments that you can open up and crawl into and then close up, almost like a little

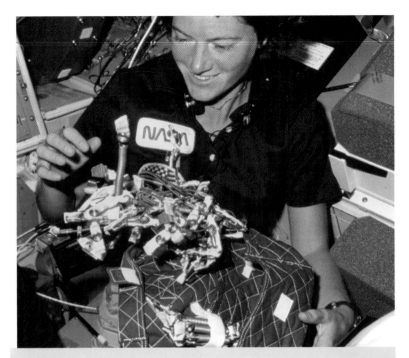

Sally Ride opens a bag of "worms"—springs, clips, bungee cords, and Velcro used to secure the astronauts while they are sleeping. If the astronauts are not strapped into their sleeping bags, they will float freely around the cabin. Ride preferred free-floating sleep and chose not to use the worms.

bedroom. Some astronauts sleep in sleeping bags that are Velcroed into one of the walls in the shuttle. It's easy to sleep floating around—it's very comfortable. But you have to be careful that you don't float into somebody or something!"

Astronauts commonly wear earplugs and eye masks to block out sound and light while sleeping. Since the shuttle orbited Earth every ninety minutes, the crew saw sixteen sunsets and sunrises every twenty-four hours. These very short days were confusing to their internal clocks, the natural mechanisms in humans that tell us when it is time to sleep and when it is time to wake up.

The food the astronauts ate while on the shuttle was also unique and took some getting used to. Astronaut food has improved dramatically since the early days of manned spaceflight. "A lot of it is like food that you'd take on a camping trip," describes Ride in the Scholastic.com interview. "With some of it, you need to add water to reconstitute it. And some of it is regular packaged food. We carried a loaf of bread and a jar of peanut butter on my flight."

All in all, the small shuttle kitchen contained an amazing selection—twenty different drinks and seventy-five varieties of food. Some of it was dehydrated and some was freeze-dried. Other food was fresh, however, like nuts and granola bars. Eating took some time, and the crew tried not to let crumbs escape and float around the

THE ZERO-GRAVITY WORKOUT

For reasons not yet clearly understood, astronauts lose bone mass more quickly in zero gravity than on Earth. Muscle loss is also common due to the fact that the body's muscles are not meeting the same resistance that they experience in Earth's heavy atmosphere. When our bodies strain against the weight of gravity, they develop stronger muscles and bones. To guard against excessive bone and muscle loss during extended missions, astronauts must exercise while in space. Each one of the crew members on the *Challenger* spent some time exercising during the six-day mission. Sometimes they did this on a treadmill, stationary bike, or rowing machine. Other times they simply tossed a bag of jelly beans back and forth.

cabin. If crumbs or liquid drops got stuck in sensitive machinery, a serious mishap could occur. All liquids were stored in closed containers with straws, much like the juice boxes sold in stores. Food was eaten on trays that were strapped to the crew members' laps. The food had extra seasonings on it because

The crew of STS-7 pose for an in-flight portrait. From left to right are Norman Thagard, mission specialist; Robert Crippen, crew commander; Sally Ride, mission specialist; and John Fabian, mission specialist. Seated in front is Frederick Hauck, pilot.

astronauts in space commonly have stuffy noses and cannot taste flavors as well as they can on Earth.

Returning to Earth

Sally Ride returned from her first trip to space on June 24, 1983. Although the *Challenger* was scheduled to land back at Cape Canaveral, bad weather in Florida forced it to land at a runway at California's Edwards Air Force Base instead. This was quite a disappointment for the thousands of people—including Ride's parents and President Ronald Reagan—who were waiting in Florida to welcome the astronauts home. As a result, only a few people were on hand at Edwards to greet the team when they landed. Ride's mother, Joyce, could not help but feel frustrated. She and Dale had traveled all the way to Florida to see their daughter's return, only to learn that she would actually land back in California, thousands of miles away. Ironically, they live less then a two-hour drive from Edwards Air Force Base.

Getting accustomed to being back in gravity once again takes a while, according to Ride. In an interview, Ride said that the transition from space to Earth is challenging. "Your heart rate doubles . . . You turn your head and the whole room spins, your arms and legs feel very heavy, you feel like the book that you were just able to float in front of you now weighs 300 pounds [136 kg] . . . The reason they don't open the hatch early and let the crew out is because the crew literally could not walk down the stairs" (as quoted in Camp's *Sally Ride*).

Though the first few moments of readjustment to Earth's gravity are difficult, the human body tends to bounce back pretty quickly. "For the first twenty minutes or so, it's a very strange feeling because your body adapts very well to weightlessness," she says in the Scholastic.com interview. "And so being back on Earth is an odd feeling. It takes a little while to get used to it and to get your muscles and your balance system working correctly again. But for most astronauts," she continues in the Hurwitzes' *Sally Ride*, "it only takes twenty to thirty minutes to get back to the point where it's easy to walk down the stairs from the shuttle and to walk in a straight line looking normal.

The space shuttle *Challenger* touched down on a dry lake bed at Edwards Air Force Base, in California, on June 24, 1983. STS-7 had lasted 147 hours. Sally Ride's successful spaceflight created opportunities for many more female astronauts in NASA. She herself would return to space within a year.

You might not feel normal for a day or two, but it's a pretty quick adjustment."

After the crew of the *Challenger* had safely landed back on Earth, they each received a phone call of congratulations from President Reagan. He took a moment to give a special message to the first American woman in space. "You were," he stated to Ride, "the best person for the job."

Ride was very satisfied with her performance on her first shuttle flight. "I was just very proud of being able to be a part of that mission, to be a part of that crew, to accomplish what I was supposed to accomplish, to fulfill my role on the mission and to have people—other members of the crew, other people at NASA, and the public—recognize that," she says in *Great American Astronauts*. Ride enjoyed her spaceflight thoroughly and recognized its central importance as a personal milestone. She remarks, "The thing I'll remember most about the flight is that it was fun. In fact, I'm sure it was the most fun that I'll ever have in my life."

CHAPTER 5

A RETURN TO SPACE AND A FAREWELL

After Sally Ride returned from her first shuttle flight into space, she found herself at the center of frenzied media attention— a position that she found quite uncomfortable. "I was not prepared for it," she says in reference to the publicity. "I knew that I was going to do a lot of interviews. I knew that there was a lot of publicity surrounding the flight, but I was not prepared for the avalanche. People stopped me on the street." She adds, "I was recognized everywhere. I basically spent most of my time over the next several months speaking to various groups, doing interviews, and

After their landing at Edwards Air Force Base on June 24, 1983, the STS-7 crew attends a press conference. Seated from left are Norman Thagard, John Fabian, Sally Ride, Frederick Hauck, and Robert Crippen.

doing things that were not really related—things that I was not used to doing" (as quoted in her interview with Cay Butler).

Ride was seen as a role model not only for young girls but also for feminists (people who believe in and strive for equal rights and opportunities for women). Even though Ride did not like being in the spotlight, she did appreciate the opportunity to inspire young girls by encouraging them to develop their skills and pursue their dreams.

Ride was scheduled to return to space on her second shuttle flight in a year and a half. In addition to preparing for the next mission, she also traveled throughout the United States, giving presentations on NASA and the shuttle program. She was also kept extremely busy going to ceremonies and receiving awards and other honors. In the months following her return from space, Ride was honored with everything from receiving the key to New York City by Mayor Edward Koch and being featured on the cover of *Ms. Magazine* (a feminist news and issues magazine) to running a leg of the 1984 Olympic Torch Relay and making a guest appearance with Oscar the Grouch on *Sesame Street*. She refused most invitations to speak to groups if she was the only astronaut invited; she much preferred going to events that included her fellow crew members.

Ride's Return to Space

Despite this busy round of appearances and media events, Ride remained focused on getting ready for her next shuttle flight in October 1984. The preparation felt somewhat easier this time around because she had already gone on one mission and had a better idea of what to expect. She reviewed flight data and practiced skills like parachute jumps, firefighting, water rescue, flight training, and robotic arm maneuvers. During this period of preparation and training, a number of other space shuttles were being sent into space. The STS-8 mission carried Guion Bluford Jr., the first African American astronaut to travel to space. Three months before Ride's second shuttle trip, on August 30, 1984, her then husband, Steven Hawley, finally got his chance to experience spaceflight on the shuttle *Discovery*.

On the morning of October 5, 1984, it was Sally Ride's turn once again. Mission STS 41–G, NASA's 100th spaceflight, launched from Florida's Kennedy Space Center. The *Challenger* remained in orbit until October 13, a total of 197 hours in space. Once again Ride served as mission specialist alongside commander Robert Crippen. Her new crewmates included pilot Jon McBride, aeronautical engineer David Leestma, Australian oceanographer Paul Scully-Power, Canadian payload specialist

Astronauts Kathryn Sullivan *(left)* and Sally Ride check their watches before takeoff of the space shuttle *Challenger* on October 5, 1984. Both women were flying on mission STS 41-G, NASA's 100th manned spaceflight. This picture was taken in the orbiter access arm, which is a passageway that leads directly to the shuttle crew compartment.

Marc Garneau, and another woman, geologist Dr. Kathryn Sullivan. In an amazing coincidence, the two women discovered that they had been schoolmates twenty-seven years earlier in California. While talking together one day, they discovered they had been in the first grade at Havenhurst Elementary School in California at the same time.

The STS 41–G contained the largest crew ever sent to space aboard the shuttle. "We bumped into each other a lot, spilled each other's food a lot," Ride recalls in the Hurwitzes' *Sally Ride*. "We came back and recommended that seven was really the maximum crew size without a space module or

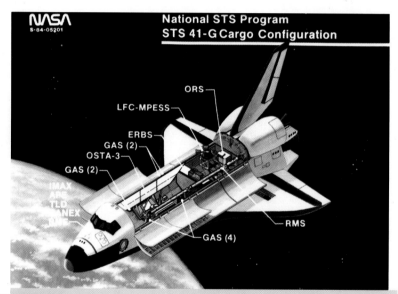

This is an artist's conception of the space shuttle's cargo bay during STS 41-G. Labeled are various experiments and cargo, known as payload. Some of the payload includes getaway specials (GAS; satellites to be released into space), the orbital refueling system (ORS), and an IMAX camera.

bigger living space." On this flight, the *Challenger* featured new technology, including upgraded radar and equipment that measured air pollution. It also carried a satellite designed to study Earth's weather patterns, especially the greenhouse effect (the gradual warming of the planet due to a buildup of gases that trap heat in the atmosphere). Various components of an orbital refueling system (ORS) were connected and tested, proving it was possible for satellites to be refueled while still in orbit. During the mission, Dr. Sullivan became the first American woman to perform a space walk.

Though the shuttle flight was clearly a success, it was not without its problems. On the first day of the mission, Ride tried to launch the weather satellite with the robotic arm and ran into a problem. The springs and hinges on the satellite's solar panels had frozen. Because the panels provided the satellite with energy to power its instruments, it could not be launched into orbit until the panels had thawed. Quickly, Ride came up with a solution to the problem: move the shuttle so that the cargo bay would be in direct sunlight. It worked, and soon the satellite was successfully sent on its way.

Above: An astronaut performs a space walk in the open cargo bay of the space shuttle. Earth can be seen beyond the shuttle's tail. The robotic arm is visible in the picture's upper right corner. *Inset:* Kathryn Sullivan uses binoculars to gaze at Earth from the shuttle window during STS 41-G.

Deaths in the NASA Family

After Ride returned from her second trip to space, she was once again treated like a celebrity. The U.S. Department of Labor minted two gold medallions bearing her image. Disneyland included her in their traditional Salute to American Heroes celebration. The American Institute of Public Service gave her their Jefferson Award. In addition, she was given the fourth annual Meridian Award, a citation handed out annually on the Merv Griffin television show. It was given to those who accomplished impressive goals, both professionally and personally.

On January 28, 1986, as Sally Ride was preparing for her third shuttle mission, NASA suffered one of the worst disasters in the history of the manned space program. The space shuttle *Challenger* exploded seventy-three seconds after liftoff. All seven crew members were killed instantly: commander Francis R. Scobee; pilot Michael J. Smith; mission specialists Judith A. Resnik, Ellison Onizuka, and Ronald E. McNair; payload specialist Gregory Jarvis; and civilian teacher Sharon Christa McAuliffe.

It was a devastating blow to the space program and to the small community of astronauts. Ride lost friends and colleagues on *Challenger*. "I have five very good friends who were on that flight," she says in *Portraits of Great American Scientists*. "Four astronauts that came in the same astronaut class that I did, whom I had worked with for eight years. So, I knew them very well. The most important part of the accident to me is losing some very good friends. It was very hard."

All shuttle flights were halted after the explosion until an investigation into the causes of the *Challenger* disaster was completed and any necessary improvements to the shuttle program and equipment were made. "[The accident] had a very sobering effect on NASA, and it had NASA rethink the safety requirements and procedures," says Ride in *Portraits of Great American Scientists*. "It put more focus back on safety, more focus on testing and reliability. And of course, there was not any space shuttle flights for almost three years after the *Challenger* accident."

In the wake of the *Challenger* disaster, President Ronald Reagan set up a special commission to sift

Top: The space shuttle *Challenger* explodes shortly after liftoff on January 28, 1986, killing all seven crew members. *Bottom:* This is a portrait of the lost crew of the *Challenger*. *Bottom row, left to right:* Michael Smith, Francis Scobee, and Ronald McNair. *Top row, left to right:* Ellison Onizuka, Sharon Christa McAuliffe, Gregory Jarvis, and Judith Resnik.

through all the data gathered concerning the explosion. The commission was then to draft a report explaining exactly what happened, as well as suggesting any necessary changes and improvements to the shuttle program. Former secretary of state William Rogers headed the group. Other commission members included former astronaut Neil Armstrong (the first human to walk on the Moon), former test pilot Chuck Yeager, scientists, teachers, businesspeople, and one working astronaut—Sally Ride.

The Rogers Commission was given 120 days to complete its report. They studied videotapes, photographs, and shuttle debris. They interviewed more than 160 people and went through 122,000 pages of information. All in all, more than 6,000 people were involved in the investigation. In June 1986, Ride and the other commission members issued a 256-page report outlining exactly what caused the explosion (a gas leak in the right solid rocket booster caused by a faulty O-ring seal) and outlined a number of new safety precautions that needed to be made for future flights.

In 1986, Sally Ride was appointed to the Rogers Commission. Pictured at bottom is the first meeting on February 6, 1986. In the front row sit Neil Armstrong *(second from left)*, the first man to walk on the Moon; William Rogers *(center)*, the commission chairman; and Sally Ride. At top, Ride and Rogers examine evidence.

An Empty Sky

Not only did the *Challenger* disaster have a negative effect on the space program, it also temporarily dampened Ride's enthusiasm for spaceflight. Before she left on her second shuttle flight, she had said, "My intention after the flight is to come back to the astronaut's office and get back in line and try and fly again. I'd like to do it as many times as NASA will let me." Before the *Challenger* disaster, Ride was scheduled to be the mission specialist on STS 61-M, her third shuttle mission. Following the tragedy and her long, hard work on the Rogers Commission, however, she no longer wanted to go, stating, "I'm not ready to fly again. I think there are very few astronauts who are ready to fly again now" (as quoted in the *Houston Chronicle*).

In her memoir, *To Space and Back*, Ride dedicated the book to the lost *Challenger* crew, writing, "On January 28, 1986, this book was almost ready to go to the printer, when the unthinkable happened. The space shuttle *Challenger* exploded one minute after liftoff. After the accident I thought a lot about the book and whether or not I wanted to change any part of it. I decided that nothing except the dedication and the words I write here should be changed."

Eventually, the remaining shuttle fleet was cleared to return to space, and the shuttle program enjoyed fourteen years of mostly problem-free spaceflight before disaster would strike again.

LIFE AFTER NASA

After Ride finished her work with the Rogers Commission, she was assigned to serve as special assistant for long-range strategic planning at NASA headquarters in Washington, D.C. While there, she published a sixty-three-page report entitled "Leadership and America's Future in Space," also known as the Ride Report. The paper suggested that NASA send astronauts back to the Moon. She also encouraged the eventual manned exploration of Mars. "Settling Mars should be our eventual goal, but it should not be our next goal," Ride wrote. "A commitment to Mars could imperil NASA's plans to put a shuttle fleet back in operation and build a space station. It would also require a tripling of the agency's budget during the mid-90s" (as quoted in *American Heros of Exploration and Flight*). After her report was released publicly, James Fletcher, NASA administrator, said to her, "You have contributed strongly to a process that will determine the goals and directions of the nation's civil space activities well into the next century" (according to *American Heroes of Exploration and Flight*).

Ride went on to help create the Office of Exploration at NASA and then served as its administrator. She traveled extensively throughout Europe and gave many lectures along the way. She also promoted her books and was inducted into the National Women's Hall of Fame.

Saying Farewell to NASA

In 1987, on her thirty-sixth birthday, Ride retired from NASA. At that point, she had logged 343 hours in space. Many were surprised by her decision. "I've always wanted to go back to a university setting," she explained in the Hurwitzes' *Sally Ride*. "I've spent many happy years at Stanford as a student and a graduate. I just got the right offer." The "right offer" was a two-year fellowship with the Center for International Security and Arms Control at Stanford University in Palo Alto, California. There, she taught

Sally Ride *(second from right)* is present to witness President Bill Clinton sign a memorandum on June 17, 1997, requiring schools run by the federal government for Native Americans and military families to ban sexual discrimination. Ride is standing with a group of other prominent and successful women.

fellow scientists how weapons were used and designed. After two years at Stanford, Ride moved on to the University of California at San Diego, where she held the position of director at the California Space Institute.

Over the next eight years, Ride wrote and published more than twenty professional papers. She has continued her research at the University of California in areas of physics that include the study of lasers. In addition to her memoir, *To Space and Back*, Ride has written four nonfiction children's books, three of them co-authored with Dr. Tam O'Shaughnessy, a college professor and psychologist whom Ride has known since they were teenagers playing tennis on the same courts. With these books, the authors hope to inspire young people to take a greater interest both in space exploration and the well-being of their home planet. *The Third Planet: Exploring the Earth from Space*, Ride and O'Shaughnessy's first book together, has an ecological theme, revealing the impact that human beings have on their fragile planet. In it, Ride writes of her experiences in orbit: "Through the small windows of the Space Shuttle I looked down

Soon after the loss of the space shuttle *Columbia* on February 1, 2003, Sally Ride again found herself investigating a fatal spaceflight. She is seen here with Air Force major general John Barry, a fellow member of the Space Shuttle Columbia Accident Investigation Board.

on Earth and saw the oceans and land that make up our planet. The view was spectacular . . . By the time I returned to Earth, I had seen most of the planet. I understood how much we could learn by studying the Earth from above."

In the fall of 2003, Ride published her fifth book, entitled *Exploring Our Solar System.*

Another Shuttle Tragedy

In spring 2003, Ride was reunited with NASA, though under very sad circumstances. She was again chosen to participate in a shuttle accident investigation after the space shuttle *Columbia* broke apart during reentry on February 1, 2003, killing the entire seven-person crew. She was the only member selected who had served on both shuttle disaster boards. While the future of the shuttle program remains in doubt, Sally Ride remains a strong supporter of the space program and manned space exploration, despite the inherent dangers and inevitable loss of life. When asked about it, Ride replied, in an MSNBC.com article, "Exploration of space is dangerous. We've lost many unmanned probes in the last two to three years, and unfortunately, they will be lost. But . . . their dream must go on."

Moving Forward

Since her retirement from NASA, Ride has been responsible for establishing several organizations devoted to advancing the sciences in public schools. One of her favorite projects is EarthKAM, or Earth Knowledge Acquired by Middle School Students, an Internet-based, NASA-sponsored organization she founded. The program provides elementary, middle, and high school students with live links to shuttle missions with the help of digital cameras placed in the windows of the shuttles. These cameras allow students to shoot and download photos of Earth from space. In an article she co-authored, Ride describes the program this way: "EarthKAM is an example of a positive use of the Internet to bring a dynamic, distant learning experience to thousands of students. It's interactive, it's almost real-time, it has constantly changing and captivating variables, and it challenges students to make decisions that are time dependent."

She writes in a *Technology Source* article entitled "EarthKAM," "The EarthKAM experience is one that will stay with the participating students forever."

To help draw more women into the sciences in general—and space in particular—Ride also formed the Sally Ride Science Club, an organization that encourages young girls in elementary and middle school to become interested in the sciences. The Sally Ride Science Festivals and Sally Ride Space Camps strive to achieve this same goal of female participation and achievement in the sciences.

When asked in the Scholastic.com interview whether she would ever like to go into space again, Ride replied, "I'd like to, but I also enjoy the physics research and teaching that I do . . . and I had always planned to leave NASA after seven or eight years and go back to a career in teaching. That's very common in NASA. Most astronauts leave after ten years or so to go back to their original careers. So I would like to go back into space again, but not if it meant I have to give up the job I have now."

Although Ride would like another chance to go to space, she is glad to have put high-profile space travel behind her. The constant media

Sally Ride is inducted into the Astronaut Hall of Fame in Titusville, Florida, on June 21, 2003, twenty years after her history-making flight aboard the space shuttle *Challenger*. She is being congratulated by James Lovell, the commander of *Apollo 13*, the famously trouble-plagued spacecraft that almost did not return to Earth.

attention had always made her feel uncomfortable. "[Media attention] complicated my life considerably because I thought of myself as an astronaut and a research physicist and not as a famous person," she explains in *Portraits of Great American Scientists*. "It took some time for me to get back to the life that I wanted." Today, she is content to explore the sky and gaze down on Earth simply by piloting her own small airplane.

Sally Ride remains a role model to young people—and particularly young women—all over the world. While her days at NASA are behind her now, her faith in the space program and in today's youth is still strong. She firmly believes that our future lies with today's children and tomorrow's space exploration. Undoubtedly, her achievements will continue to serve as an inspiration for many decades and generations to come.

GLOSSARY

astrophysics The study of the physical properties of celestial bodies, such as stars, planets, and moons.

buoyancy The ability to float.

catapult To be forcibly thrown upward.

citation A commendation or written praise.

deploy To carefully place something in its proper place or where it can be most useful.

disorientation A state of confusion.

integration The bringing together of separate elements or groups of people.

ominous Foreshadowing evil or bad luck.

rigorous Difficult, demanding, and exhausting.

transition A change from one condition or state to another.

FOR MORE INFORMATION

American Astronautical Society
6352 Rolling Mill Place, Suite 102
Springfield, VA 22152-2354
(703) 866-0020
Web site: http://www.astronautical.org

Goddard Space Flight Center
Code 130, Office of Public Affairs
Greenbelt, MD 20771
(301) 286-8955
Web site: http://www.gsfc.nasa.gov

Jet Propulsion Laboratory
Mail Stop 186-113
4800 Oak Grove Drive
Pasadena, CA 91109
(818) 354-4321
Web site: http://www.jpl.nasa.gov

Johnson Space Center
Visitors Center
1601 NASA Road 1
Houston, TX 77058
(281) 244-2100
Web site: http://www.jsc.nasa.gov

Kennedy Space Center Visitor Complex
Mail Code: XA/Public Inquiries
Kennedy Space Center, FL 32899
(321) 867-5000
Web site: http://www.ksc.nasa.gov

NASA Headquarters
Information Center
Washington, DC 20546-0001
(202) 358-0000
Web site: http://www.nasa.gov

National Air and Space Museum
Seventh Street and Independence Avenue SW
Washington, DC 20560
(202) 357-2700
Web site: http://www.nasm.si.edu

National Association of Rocketry
P.O. Box 177
Altoona, WI 54720
(800) 262-4872
Web site: http://www.nar.org

Dr. Sally Ride
c/o Terry McEntee
9500 Gilman Drive, Dept. 0426
La Jolla, CA 92093-0426
e-mail: tmcentee@ucsd.edu

Space Policy Institute
1957 E Street NW, Suite 403
Washington, DC 20052
(202) 994-7292
Web site: http://www.gwu.edu/~spi

United States Strategic Command
Public Affairs
901 SAC Blvd, Suite 1A1
Offutt Air Force Base, NE 68113-6020
(402) 294-4130
Web site: http://www.spacecom.mil

U.S. Space Camp
P.O. Box 070015
Huntsville, AL 35807-7015
(800) 533-7281
(256) 721-7150
http://www.spacecamp.com

Web Sites

Due to the changing nature of Internet links, the
Rosen Publishing Group, Inc., has developed an
online list of Web sites related to the subject of
this book. This site is updated regularly. Please use
this link to access the list:

http://www.rosenlinks.com/lasb/srid

FOR FURTHER READING

Hopping, Lorraine Jean. *Sally Ride: Space Pioneer.* New York: McGraw-Hill, 2000.

Kramer, Barbara. *Sally Ride: A Space Biography.* Berkeley Heights, NJ: Enslow Publishers, Inc., 1998.

Ride, Sally, and Tam O'Shaughnessy. *The Third Planet: Exploring the Earth from Space.* New York: Crown Publishers, 1994.

Ride, Sally, and Tam O'Shaughnessy. *To Space and Back.* New York: Lothrop, Lee, and Shepard, 1986.

Taylor, Robert. *Life Aboard the Space Shuttle.* San Diego: Lucent Books, 2002.

Woodmansee, Laura. *Women Astronauts.* New York: Apogee Books, 2002.

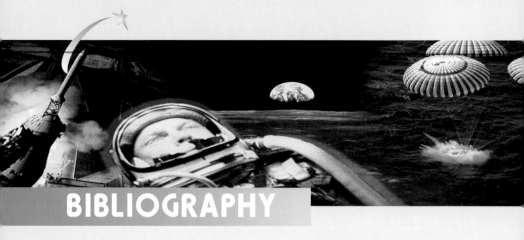

BIBLIOGRAPHY

Atkins, Jeannine. *Wings and Rockets: The Story of Women in Air and Space.* New York: Farrar, Straus & Giroux, 2003.

Briggs, Carole S. *Women in Space.* Minneapolis: Lerner Publishing Group, 1999.

Butler, Cay. "Reaching for the Stars—Interviews with Women Astronauts: Sally Ride." Association for Women in Space. Retrieved June 2003 (http://www.awis.org/m_02sprride.html).

Camp, Carole Ann. *Sally Ride: First American Woman in Space.* Berkeley Heights, NJ: Enslow Publishers, Inc., 1997.

Carreau, Mark. "Sally Ride Is Leaving NASA After Making Major Contributions." *Houston Chronicle*, September 21, 1987. Retrieved June 2003 (http://www.chron.com/content/interactive/space/archives/87/870921.html).

"Columbia Crash Hits Titusville Hard." MSNBC. com, February 3, 2003. Retrieved June 2003 (http://stacks.msnbc.com:80/local/wpbf/ a1480284.asp).

Crocker, Chris. *Great American Astronauts.* New York: Franklin Watts, Inc., 1989.

Freni, Pamela S. *Space for Women: A History of Women with the Right Stuff.* Santa Ana, CA: Seven Locks Press, 2002.

Hurwitz, Jane, and Sue Hurwitz. *Sally Ride: Shooting for the Stars.* New York: Fawcett Columbine Books, 1989.

Jenkins, Dennis R. *Space Shuttle: The History of the National Space Transportation System: The First 100 Missions.* North Branch, MN: Specialty Press and Publishers Wholesalers, Inc., 2001.

Joelys, Kerry Mark, Gregory P. Kennedy, and David Larkin. *Space Shuttle Operator's Manual.* New York: Ballantine Books, 1988.

Lederman, Leon, and Judith Scheppler, eds. *Portraits of Great American Scientists.* New York: Prometheus Books, 2001.

Reichardt, Tony, ed. *Space Shuttle: The First 20 Years: The Astronauts' Experiences in Their Own Words.* New York: DK Publishing, 2002.

Ride, Sally, and Dennis Govoni. "EarthKAM: NASA, the Internet, and Education Working Together." Technology Source online, January 1999. Retrieved June 2003 (http://ts.mivu.org/default.asp?show=article&id=55).

Ride, Sally, and Tam O'Shaughnessy. *To Space and Back*. New York: Lothrop, Lee, and Shepard, 1986.

"Sally Ride Interview." Scholastic.com, November 20, 1998. Retrieved June 2003 (http://teacher.scholastic.com/space/sts7/interview.htm).

Schraff, Anne E. *American Heroes of Exploration and Flight*. Berkeley Heights, NJ: Enslow Publishers, Inc., 1995.

Thompson, Milton O., and Curtis Peebles. *Flying Without Wings: NASA Lifting Bodies and the Birth of the Space Shuttle*. Washington, DC: Smithsonian Institution Press, 1999.

Ward, Ingaret. *The Greatest Adventure*. Sydney, Australia: C. Pierson Publishers, 1994.

Woodmansee, Laura S. *Women Astronauts*. Toronto, ON: Apogee Books, 2002.

INDEX

About the Author

Tamra Orr is a full-time writer living in Portland, Oregon. She is the home-schooling mother of four and has written more than a dozen nonfiction books for children and families.

Photo Credits

Cover, pp. 1, 39, 40, 43, 44, 49, 51, 52, 54, 60, 65, 66, 67, 70, 79, 80, 82 (inset) courtesy of NASA; pp. 4–5, 11, 28, 31, 34, 57, 58, 87 © Bettmann/Corbis; p. 7 © H. Armstrong Roberts/Corbis; p. 13 © James A. McDivitt/ Time Life Pictures/Getty Images; p. 19 © Classmates.com; p. 26 © David Butow/Corbis Saba; pp. 73, 85 © Corbis; p. 76 © Douglas Kirkland/Corbis; p. 82 © NASA/Roger Ressmeyer/Corbis; pp. 92, 94 © AP/Wide World Photos; p. 98 © Reuters NewMedia Inc./Corbis.

Designer: Les Kanturek; Editor: John Kemmerer